Encounters

Early Images

of Canada's

Aboriginal Peoples

From the
Library Collections of the
Geological Survey of Canada

John A. Stevens

Published by

GENERAL STORE
PUBLISHING HOUSE

1 Main Street, Burnstown, Ontario, Canada K0J 1G0
1-800-465-6072 or Fax: (613) 432-7184
© 1996
Geological Survey of Canada
General Store Publishing House

General Store Publishing House gratefully acknowledges the assistance of the Ontario Arts Council.

Canadian Cataloguing in Publication Data
Stevens, John A., 1949
                Encounters: early images of Canada's aboriginal
peoples, from the library collections of the
Geological Survey of Canada

Includes bibliographical references
ISBN 1-896182-46-1
Printed and bound in Canada

        1. Native peoples—Canada. I. Title
E78.C2S693 1996   305.897071   C96-900304-8

Layout and Design by
EarthLore Communications Canada

First Printing 1996

Introduction

The Geological Survey of Canada began sending survey parties to explore, map and document this vast country more than 150 years ago. Their mandate went far beyond registering landforms and mineral deposits; geologists in the field were instructed to observe and record virtually everything they came across.

Almost as soon as photography was invented, they began taking cameras, with their fragile glass plates, into the wilderness with them. As a result, the Survey has amassed a priceless collection of over half a million images preserving a record of the land they have studied, and relating it to the life and natural processes it supported.

Among those thousands of photographs is a rich archive of images of Canada's Aboriginal peoples. The earliest reveal individuals, families and nations in transition; behind them a shattering collision with expansionist European civilization, before them an unrecognisable future in which their place is uncertain. These photographs constitute an irreplacable record of an encounter between

peoples, and the best of them recognise and salute the heart and soul of the stranger.

Because of the timing of the introduction of photography and the Survey's exploration of the country, the collection's greatest depth is in images from western Canada and the Arctic.

This book provides a small sample of the collection, demonstrating its range of subject and detail. It also provides a list of materials in the Survey's library for reading in anthropology, archaeology, ethnography, exploration, history, policy and politics.

The names of many of the people in these photographs have been lost. If you can identify any of them, we would be very pleased to hear from you.

The Geological Survey of Canada invites you to make use of its holdings for research, educational, artistic and commercial purposes. You will find information about access to the collections at the back of the book.

Editor's note:
The text accompanying the photographs is presented exactly as it was originally written by Geological Survey officers. In some cases they used terms which convey attitudes and assumptions about native people that are no longer acceptable. In the interests of historical accuracy, however, we have left the text unaltered.

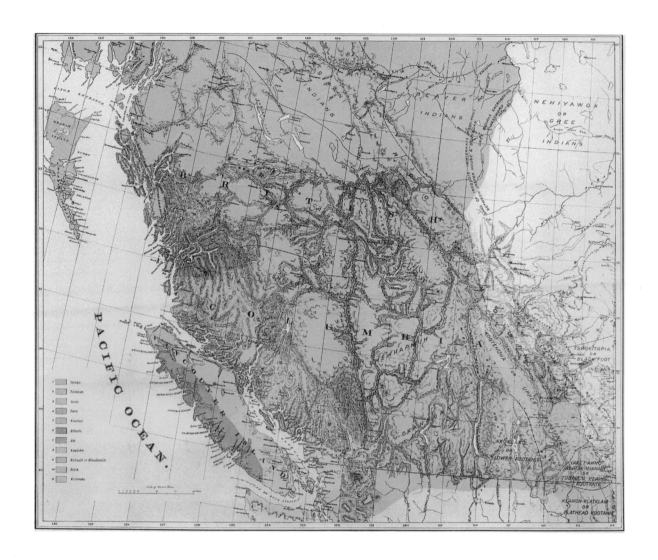

Map showing the distribution of
the Indian Tribes of British Columbia
W.F. Tolmie and G.M. Dawson, 1883

Skidegate Indian Village

Queen Charlotte Islands, British Columbia

G.M. Dawson, 1878

The door is to one side of the middle, & not through the bottom of the totem post as in the older fashioned buildings.... The floor boarded, with the exception of a square space of earth in the middle for the fire. The Chattels of the family piled here & there in heaps along the walls, leaving the greater part of the interior Clear. The dancers... occupy the front end, the audience the sides & further (in)end of the house. The smoke from the fire, — which the only light — escaping by wide openings in the roof. The Audience nearly fill the building, squatting in various attitudes on the floor, & Consisting of Men women & children of all ages. Their faces all turned forward & expressive of various emotions lit up by the fire. (Skidegate village about 25 houses & some 53 totem posts.)...

...The performers in this instance about twenty in number... all wore head dresses, variously constructed of cedar bark rope ornamented with feathers &c. or as in one case with a bristling circle of the whiskers of the Sea-lion. Shoulder girdles made of Cedar-bark rope, variously ornamented and coloured, with tassels etc. very common. One man wore gaiters covered with fringes of strung puffin bills which rattled as he moved. Nearly if not all held sprigs of fresh spruce, & were covered about the head with downey feathers which also filled the warm atmosphere of the house. Rattles were also in order. Different from the rest, however, five women who stood in front, dressed with some uniformity. Several having the peculiarly beautiful mountain goat shawls which are purchased from the Main-land Indians. The head-dresses of these women were also pretty nearly the same consisting of small mask faces carved in wood and inlaid with haliotis shell, these Attached to Cedar bark and built around with gay feathers &c. stood above the forehead... in the heat of the dance. I suppose the Indians may yet almost imagine the old palmy days when hundreds crowded the village and nothing had eclipsed the grandeur of their ceremonies and doings... to remain.

— George M. Dawson,
The Journals of George M. Dawson: British Columbia, 1875-1878, Vol. 2, 1878

following page
Group of Blood Indians,
Fort Whoop Up
G.M. Dawson, 1881

Cumshewa Indian village
Queen Charlotte Islands, British Columbia
G.M. Dawson, 1878

A few years ago the firm to which the *Active* belongs established a station on the south side of Southampton, and imported a number of the Big Island natives. These natives, being provided with modern rifles, soon killed off or frightened away the deer in the neighbourhood. The old inhabitants of the island (Sagdlingmuit) being armed only with bow and arrows and spears, were unable to compete with the better armed strangers, and as a result the entire tribe, who numbered 68 souls in 1900, died of starvation and disease during the winter of 1902.

— A.P. Low, *The Cruise of the Neptune*, 1903-4

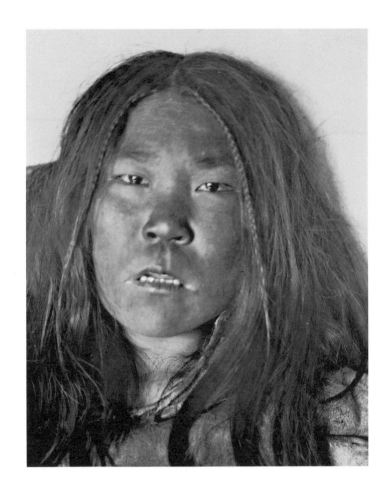

The murderer's wife
Hudson Bay
A.P. Low, 1903

Cree Indian
Maple Creek, Saskatchewan
T.C. Weston, 1884

Indian house

Fort Rupert, British Columbia

G.M. Dawson, 1885

Ow-Wit, Quatsino Chief,

wife, son, son's wife and child

Quatsino, British Columbia

G.M. Dawson, 1885

Big Bear's Camp (Cree Indian)
Maple Creek, Saskatchewan
G.M. Dawson, 1883

Group of Indians
Fort George
A.P. Low, 1896

facing page:
Chief Wigamouskunk and family
Lake St. Martin, Manitoba
J.B. Tyrrell, 1888

... in pursuing this research, it has been my ambition to achieve a better understanding of the acculturation experienced by the Inuit during early contact with Europeans. In so doing, I attempt to identify the material evidence which differentiates the two cultures, to infer the time when the Labrador Inuit began to settle in the Strait of Belle Isle, and to draw some conclusions about the respective positions of European and Inuit settlements in light of the seemingly con-frontational relations between the two cultures. Finally, I discuss the cultural, social and economic factors which may have motivated the Inuit to settle in a region they had not previously occupied.

— *Reginald Auger, Labrador Inuit and Europeans in the Strait of Belle Isle: from the Written Sources to the Archaeological Evidence, 1991*

Untitled
Hudson's Bay
A.P. Low, 1899

"Harry", chief of the Aivilirmuit
Fullerton, Hudson's Bay
A.P. Low, 1903-4

Aivillik women with tattooed faces

Fullerton, Hudson's Bay

A.P. Low, 1903-4

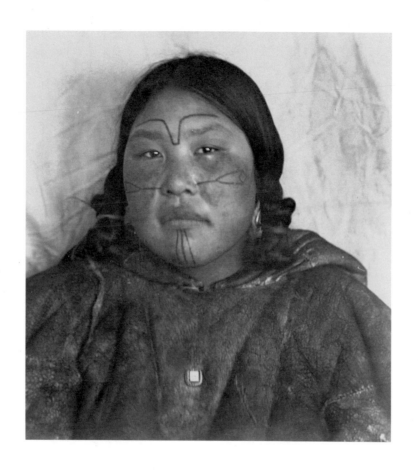

Tattooed Aivillik woman
Igluirmuit, Southampton Island, Hudson's Bay
A.P. Low, 1903-4

On the west side of Hudson bay the Kenipitus live inland, and depend entirely upon the caribou for food, clothing and fuel. A large number of these natives only leave their hunting grounds for short visits to the whalers, to renew their supplies of ammunition and tobacco, or to go to the northward to hunt the musk-ox in the spring.

The Aivilliks of that coast confine themselves chiefly to the seaboard. Their name signifies walrus hunters, and they go inland in autumn only to procure sufficient deerskins for their winter clothing.

— A.P. Low, *The Cruise of the Neptune*, 1903-4

Eskimo children
Fullerton, Hudson's Bay
A.P. Low, 1903-4

The largest single house, seen by the writer, at Cape Fullerton, was twenty-seven feet in diameter and twelve feet from the floor to the centre of the dome; it was inhabited by four families. This house was too large for the material, and the roof had to be supported by props shortly after being built; but several others, eighteen feet in diameter, showed no signs of such weakness.

— A.P. Low,
The Cruise of the Neptune, 1903-4

Inside of snowhouse at Cape Fullerton
Hudson's Bay
A.P. Low, 1903-4

Camp of Micmac Indians
Elmsdale, Nova Scotia
E.R. Faribault, 1891

Eskimos on the Neptune

Arctic

Robert Bell, 1884

previous page:

Indians

Hudson's Bay

Doctor Robert Bell, (Manitoba, 1880?)

Eskimo hunters at head of Baker Lake

Northwest Territories

J.B. Tyrrell, 1893

Eskimos in boat

Hudson's Bay, N.E.T.

A.P. Low, 1897

The natives have another boat called the
umiak or woman's boat. This is also made with
a wooden frame covered with skins, but it is
much larger than the hunting kayak of the
men. In shape it roughly resembles a large
square-ended punt, being often twenty feet
and over in length, by six feet or more across
the middle section, tapering towards the ends
to about half that width. It is made quite deep,
and is capable of carrying a very heavy load.
Usually two or more families use a single
umiak to transport their goods from place to
place, and as the poles and Big sealskin cover-
ing of each tent weigh upwards of half a ton,
the capacity of these boats can be realized.

— A.P. Low,
The Cruise of the Neptune, 1903-4

A photograph of two little native girls

J.E. Hyde, 1912

There was once a boy who used to set his snares for his living. One day he saw a track where the snow was melted, and after a while he decided to set his snares there and catch the animal that made the tracks. So he set his snares and went away. That track was the sun's track, and when the sun came by the next day, it got caught. The sun didn't rise the next day and there was steady darkness. The people began to be puzzled. "Where did you set your snare?" they asked him. He told them and they went to look. There they saw the sun caught, but no one could go near enough to loosen it. A number of animals tried to do this, but they all got burned. At last the Beaver-mouse managed to cut it with his teeth and freed it. But his teeth got burned with the heat, and so they are brown to this day, but the sun is here and we have the daylight.

— Related by Aleck Paul, second chief of Timagami band, to F.G. Speck

— *Myths and Folk-lore of the Timiskaming Algonquin and Timagami Ojibwa — GSC Memoir 71*

F.G. Speck, 1932

Indian grave (Ojibway)

Round Lake, Moss Township

William McInnes, 1891

Micmac Indians
Oldham, Nova Scotia
A. Mailhoit, 1913

The Ojibwa attributed nearly all pictographs to the Iroquois. On Lady Evelyn Lake are a number of such figures, showing animals and men in canoes.

— F.G. Speck,
Myths and Folk-lore of the Timiskaming Algonquin and Timagami Ojibwa
— GSC Memoir 71, No. 9,
Anthropological Series, 1915

Caughnawaga Indians
Quebec
A. Mailhoit, 1913

"The Iroquois used to come here to fight the Ojibwa because the Americans had driven them from their homes in the States and the Iroquois had to seek new countries beyond the settlements in the North. In their excursions, when they got far from home, they cut and painted pictures in the rocks on river and lake shores, so that their friends, if they ever penetrated so far, would know that their own people had been there before them. The characters of these pictures would tell what had happened, so that if the advance party never returned to their people, some record would at least be left behind of their journey."

— Chief Aleck Paul, 1913

Gotcheo L., a Celebrated resort of the Indians, a building of theirs existing here known as the Culla-Culla House, or Bird House, a large Crow Carved in wood, rather neatly, & painted black, adorning one gable. The Indians tell me that the [abode?] made by Bella Coola Indians, the natives here not understanding painting and decoration so well. A curious instance of mingling of customs of two now friendly tribes.

— George M. Dawson,
The Journals of George M. Dawson: British Columbia, 1875-1878, Vol. 1, 1876

Eagle Totem Pole
East end Maud Isle, British Columbia
J.D. MacKenzie, 1913

Chipewyan Indians
Fond du Lac, Lake Athabasca, Alberta
F.J. Alcock, 1914

previous page:
Indian tent
Fond du Lac, Lake Athabasca, Alberta
F.J. Alcock, 1914

Four Cree drummers at a tea dance
Fort Chipewyan, Alberta
F. Harper, 1914

Pierre Pierrot (Chipewyan) with two large coneys at
our camp, Taltson River at mouth of Pierrot Creek
Northern Alberta
F. Harper, 1914

Indian girl (Cree and Chipewyan) at our camp
at mouth of Taltson River, with birchbark basket
Northwest Territories or northern Alberta
F. Harper, 1914

Indian boy in front of teepee at Pointe-de-Grovois
Slave River, Northwest Territories
F. Harper, 1914

facing page:
Group of Chipewyans at our camp.
Taltson River at mouth of Pierrot Creek
Northwest Territories or northern Alberta
F. Harper, 1914

Half-breed boy with two Hoyt's horned larks
and a stick for striking down birds on the ground
Fort McMurray, Alberta
F. Harper, 1914

Alexander LaVivlette, a chief of the Chipewyans (3/4 Chipewyan and 1/4 French) playing checkers, he is the most distant one in the group of four

Fort Chipewyan, Alberta

F. Harper, 1914

Once a hunter was so quick of foot that when he shot his arrow at a beaver plunging into the lake from the shore, he would run down, catch the beaver by the tail before the arrow got to it, and hold it until the arrow struck. He was a fast runner indeed.

— Related by Aleck Paul, second chief of Timagami band, to F.G. Speck — *Myths and Folk-lore of the Timiskaming Algonquin and Timagami Ojibwa* — GSC Memoir 71, No. 9, Anthropological Series, 1915

Indian teepee, girl and boy
Banff, Alberta
E.M. Kindle, 1915

facing page:
James Daniell, a Saulteaux half-breed with fish just brought from his nets; also his wife and his dogs. His catch included a Goldeye (right hand), a Pike, Whitefish (left hand)
Fort Chipewyan, Alberta
F. Harper, 1914

Indian girls
Pass Reservation, Manitoba
E.L. Bruce, 1915

previous page:
Stoney Indians
Banff, Alberta
E.M. Kindle, 1915

Economically these territories were managed in a very wise
and interesting manner. The game was kept account of very
closely, so that the proprietors knew about how abundant
each kind of animal was, and hence could regulate the killing
so as not to deplete the stock. Beaver were made the object of
the most careful "farming," the numbers of occupants, old and
young, of each "cabin" being kept count of. In certain dis-
tricts, moose, or caribou, were protected during one year,
in another district, the next year. The killing of game was
regulated by each family according to its own rules.

— F.G. Speck, *Family Hunting Territories and Social Life of Various Algonkian Bands of
the Ottawa Valley*, GSC Memoir 70, No. 8, Anthropological Series, 1915

Robert Pier, Ojibway, hunting on Mattagami Lake
with his wife, daughters, and daughters-in-law
Quebec
C.H. Cook, 1915

Chipewyan encampment on Taltson River at mouth of Pierrot Creek

Northern Alberta

F. Harper, 1914

For the first year or two at least a marriage is considered a kind of trial in which the young couple discover whether they can adapt themselves to each other and live together harmoniously or not. The girl may leave her husband at any time and return to her parents, taking with her all her possessions; but in that case, the bride-price, if any has been paid, must be restored to her former husband.... It often happens that a girl is divorced, or divorces herself, two or three times within a year. On the other hand, instances of genuine affection are not at all uncommon, even before a child is born to cement the union. Avranna and Milukkattak might often be seen stretched out on the bed-skins in their hut, pressing noses and caressing each other, wholly oblivious of the presence of other natives around them. Milukkattak would go out hunting with him, and sealing too at times, so that they might not be separated for a single hour. In February, 1916, Avranna accompanied me on a visit to the Bathurst Inlet natives. Milukkattak wanted to come too, but as her time of delivery was near it was thought advisable for her to remain behind. She entreated me to look after her husband, not allow any eastern woman to seduce his affections but to bring him safely back again. We were absent only a few weeks, but Avranna was worried about his wife all the time; he was certainly the happiest man in all the country when he joined her again and saw a little baby face peering over her shoulder.

— Diamond Jenness,
Canadian Arctic Expedition, 1913-18

Eskimo man
Coronation Gulf
G.H. Wilkens, 1913-1916

Eskimo woman, Copper Eskimo
G.H. Wilkens, 1913-1916

facing page:
Kaptane scraping skin, Copper Eskimo
G.H. Wilkens, 1913-1916

Eskimo man

Coronation Gulf

G.H. Wilkens, 1913-1916

Tree River natives coming
down river October 16th, 1915
J.J. O'Neill, 1915

Eskimo cache at Cape Wallaston

Bathurst Inlet

J.J. O'Neill, 1913-1916

Eskimo grave at King Point
J.R. Cox, 1914

Marriage involves no subjection on the part of the woman. She has her own sphere of activity, and within that she is as supreme as her husband is in his. All important matters, such as the migrating to another settlement, are discussed between them before any decision is taken. Both within and without the house she behaves as the equal of the men. Her voice is heard in the dance-house when any deliberations are in progress, even in the hunting field when caribou are sighted and a drive is to be organized. Some of the women are shamans, and so obtain a considerable influence in the communities to which they belong.

— Diamond Jenness,
Canadian Arctic Expedition, 1913-18

Eskimo woman shaping sealskin for slippers
Northwest Territories
J.R. Cox, 1916

Eskimo children show little respect for their elders in the manner to which we are accustomed. They address them as equals, and join in any conversation that may be taking place, not hesitating to interrupt or even correct their parents. Often they have nicknames for their elders which they will use to their very faces; thus Kanneyuk would sometimes call her mother "the woman with the wide mouth". Yet they do show a certain amount of deference, and a child will generally do what it is told, however unwilling. If it disobeys, an elder is sure to chide it and lecture it on the duty of children; the shame of public disapproval is sufficient in most cases to produce submission.

— Diamond Jenness, *Canadian Arctic Expedition*, 1913-18

Atigeriak and Aga
Kogluktuarluk
J.R. Cox, 1915

Group of Copper Eskimos

J. R. Cox, 1915

The Copper Eskimo used the three-piece drilling set, found among other Eskimo tribes. The bow was of bone, generally the rib of a musk-ox or caribou; a hole was drilled in each end for the attachment of the sealskin cord. The stem or spindle was nearly always of wood, though bone was used occasionally and ivory when it was procurable. To prevent the wood from splitting, a bead of bone, antler or musk-ox horn was added to it, either as a cap or by splicing. All the drills I saw had points of iron, which had long been current in very small quantities; copper perhaps was used earlier, and stone, although the natives seemed to have no recollection of the stone drill points.

— Diamond Jenness,
Canadian Arctic Expedition, 1913-18

Copper Eskimo drilling bone with bow drill
Coppermine River
J.R. Cox, 1916

Manigurin, Kakoktak and Ikey

Algaq

J.R. Cox, 1916

In order to guard against the occurrence of snow-blindness, the Eskimos wear a very ingenious contrivance, in the form of wooden goggles. These are neatly carved so as to fit over the nose, and close in to the sockets of the eyes. Instead of coloured glass, which the Eskimos have no means of getting, these goggles are made with horizontal slits, just wide enough to allow the wearer to see through. Thus the excess of light is excluded, while the sight is not entirely obstructed.

— J.W. Tyrrell,
Across the Sub-Arctics of Canada: A Journey of 3,200 Miles by Canoe and Snow-Shoe Through the Barren-Lands, 1897

Copper Eskimo Group

J.R. Cox, 1916

Oluksak and his three wives
Mouth of Coppermine River
J.R. Cox, 1916

Roxy and wife (hoods up)

J.R. Cox, 1916

While occupied with building the snow houses the Inuit suddenly abandoned their work and began with all haste to build a small, separate snow house. It was very quickly finished and soon after she had entered the house Netsilik Joe's wife gave birth to a son; she had walked twenty miles that day hauling a sledge.

— Heinrich Klutschak,

Overland to Starvation Cove: With the Inuit in Search of Franklin, 1878-1880

Copper Eskimo building snow village
Bernard Harbour
J.R. Cox, 1915

Manigurin and baby

Itayuk

J.R. Cox, 1916

Small Eskimo girl (Ihumalak)
Mouth of Coppermine River
J.R. Cox, 1916

Summer migration

Coppermine River

K.G. Chipman, 1913-1916

A migration of a whole community is a wonderful sight. In the autumn, when the Eskimos are moving out to their sealing-grounds, they have to start with their sleds before daylight in order to reach their destinations before dark. Time is everything at that season of the year, and often half the journey is made in twilight. In spring, on the other hand, there is no need for haste, for the air is mild and pleasant, and the daylight as long as the darkness has been in the winter.

— Diamond Jenness,
Canadian Arctic Expedition, 1913-18

Copper Eskimo Pasking

K.G. Chipman, 1913-1916

The matter, however, that constitutes the main bond of union and interest in these groups is the family hunting territory, in which all the male members share the right of hunting and fishing... Hunting outside of one's inherited territory was punishable occasionally by death.... Permission, however, could be obtained by a man to hunt in another's territory. This happened frequently as an exchange of courtesies between families when the game supply of one or the other became impoverished.... When it was necessary in travelling to pass through another family territory, permission was generally sought at the owner's headquarters before passing on, and if by necessity game had been killed to sustain life, the pelts were carried to the owners or delivered to them by a friend. This gave the proprietors the right in the future to do the same in the territory of their trespassers. These arrangements were matters of tradition and were remembered in detail by the families concerned.

— F.G. Speck,
Family Hunting Territories and Social Life of Various Algonkian Bands of the Ottawa Valley, GSC Memoir 70, No. 8, Anthropological Series, 1915

Indians with captured mud hen
Ontario
R.C. McDonald, 1917

81

All the dances on the preceding day had
been of the *pisik* type, the dancer, that is, had
also beaten the drum. But on this occasion
several of the *aton* type were given. Higilak
began the change. On entering the ring she
rapped the drum a few times to get her song
well started, then handed the instrument to
Allikammik and the stick to Kunana, and
executed a wild kind of jig, waving her arms
in the air and swinging around on both feet,
only roughly in time with the music. Sometimes she would call on the spectators to sing
louder, and swell the chorus herself with her
voice; at other times she would utter whoops
and shouts of joy, interspersed with remarks
to the singers, remarks such as, "Aren't we
glad the Kanghiryuarmuit have come."

— Diamond Jenness,
Canadian Arctic Expedition, 1913-18

Anivyunna, singing
G.H. Wilkins, 1913-1916

previous page:
Indian camp at Ramparts
E.M. Kindle, 1919

Indian celebrations during Scottish games at Banff
Alberta
B.R. MacKay, 1927

Montagnais Indians
Seven Islands, Quebec
W.F. James, 1933

facing page:
Wise old woman
Diamond Jenness, 1934

Montagnais, note cap on woman to left which is
made in red and blue seems to be characteristic of
the tribe. Cross is commonly worn on a cord
around the neck among these members of the tribe
who are Roman Catholic
Seven Islands, Quebec
W.F. James, 1933

Indians (Montagnais) at annual Mission
Mackenzie, in centre is the newly elected chief
Seven Islands, Quebec
W.F. James, 1933

The Rev. Mr. Girling tells me of a very touching custom that he witnessed on two or three occasions. He was travelling along the coast with an Eskimo from Bathurst Inlet when the native met his aged mother, whom he had not seen for many years. The old woman lifted up the front of her coat, exposing her breast, and her son reverently stooped down and touched it with his lips.

— Diamond Jenness,
Canadian Arctic Expedition, 1913-18

Voisey sisters showing intricate designs of Eskimo parka decorations
Repulse Bay, Northwest Territories
D.A. Nichols, 1940

Indian camp
Shoal River, Manitoba
J.B. Tyrrell, 1889

previous page:
Indians at Mastissini, Quebec
A.P. Low, 1884

We soon found we were not the only ones waiting, and that anxiously, for the arrival of the scows from the south. The entire population at Fort MacMurray was in a state of famine. Supplies at the post, having been insufficient for the demand, had become exhausted, and the Indians who had come in to barter their furs were thus far unable to obtain food in exchange, and were obliged, with their families, to subsist upon the few rabbits that might be caught in the woods... At one Cree camp visited I witnessed a most pitiable sight. There was a whole family of seven or eight persons seated on the ground about their smoking camp-fire, but without one morsel of food, while children, three or four years old, were trying to satisfy their cravings at the mother's breast.

— J.W. Tyrrell,
Across the Sub-Arctics of Canada: A Journey of 3,200 Miles by Canoe and Snow-Shoe Through the Barren-Lands, 1897

The natives about Cumberland gulf and along the west side of Hudson Bay, who are employed by the whalers, are gradually giving up the use of the kayak, and now do their hunting and travelling with the whaleboats, which are supplied to them by the whaling vessels. Each vessel at the end of her voyage generally leaves all spare boats behind. These are distributed among the natives, and the result is that nearly every family possesses a boat. The Aivilliks and Kenipitus, of the west coast of Hudson Bay, still make use of the kayaks for inland hunting, but the Cumberland people take their whaleboats into the interior.

— A.P. Low,
The Cruise of the Neptune, 1903-4

Eskimo kayaks covered with caribou skin

Kazon River

J.B. Tyrrell, 1893

The year begins with the lengthening days of January, and this is usually a period of hard times, lasting for a couple of months.... The ice along the coast in January does not extend far from the shore, and the seals keep in the open water, where they can only be killed by being shot from the edge of the ice. This is a very uncertain subsistence for the native, owing to the storms of the season, which either break the ice from the shore, or crowd its edge with small floating cakes, forming an impassable barrier to the open water. If a good supply of deer-meat has not been laid during the fall, periods of starvation are now frequent... the party, usually consisting of two or more families, travels slowly southward along the shore ice, a woman often walking ahead of the dogs to encourage them. The men wander about on the ice in search of seal-holes, and occasionally secure a seal while on the journey. In the evening a halt is made, and the men build a small snowhouse with blocks cut from a convenient bank. These small houses, built only for the night, seldom exceed nine or ten feet in diameter, and it is only when a considerable stay is expected that larger houses are built.

— A.P. Low,
The Cruise of the Neptune, 1903-4

Total native population of Ellesmere Island
Craig Harbour
D.A. Nichols, 1937

previous page:
Indian boys and pack dogs
H.S. Bostock, 1946

Arctic winter quarters

E.A. Schiller, 1964

With the advent of June, the snow begins to melt, and soon after the land becomes bare. This is a period of trial for the house-wife; the warmth causes the roof of the snow-houses to leak, and they can only be kept up by a daily patching with loose snow, while the ground is not sufficiently bare for the erection of the summer tent; it becomes a constant fight with the heat and water, terminated only by the roof falling in.

— A.P. Low,
The Cruise of the Neptune, 1903-4

I never knew of any instance where a couple separated after a child was born to them. It does occur, though very rarely. One reason perhaps why it seldom happens is that the wife can still claim to be supported by her husband. Even in childless marriages, if a man divorces his wife and takes another, the first wife still has a claim on him.

— Diamond Jenness,
Canadian Arctic Expedition, 1913-18

Lake trout caught in net at foot of Port Epworth, Mingeouk for scale

J.J. O'Neill, 1913-1916

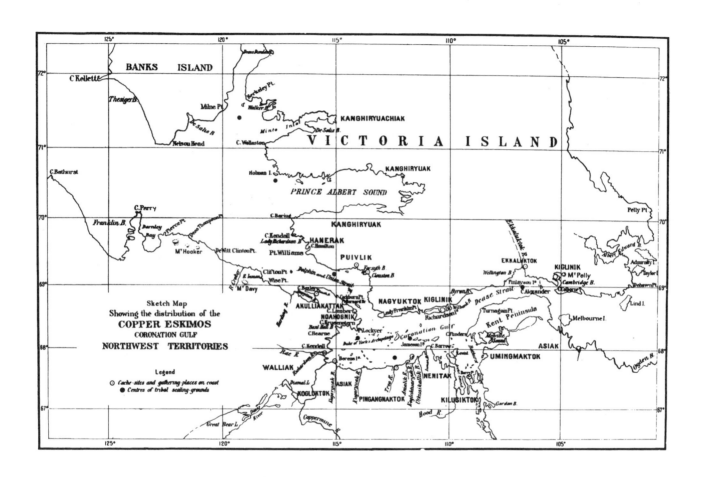

Sketch map showing the distribution of the Copper Eskimos, Coronation Gulf region, Northwest Territories.

From *Report of the Canadian Arctic Expedition, 1913-18, Volume XII: The Copper Eskimos*

Selected Readings

From the Library Collections of
the Geological Survey of Canada

Anthropology
& Ethnology

Bulletin (National Museum of Canada). Ottawa: Government Printing Bureau, 1913-1970. Title varies. Contains 3 subseries: Anthropological, Biological and Geographical, which have separate numbering.

Calder, Ritchie. *Men Against the Frozen North*. New York: MacMillan, 1957.

Canada Department of Indian Affairs and Northern Development. *The Canadian Indian: Yukon and Northwest Territories*. Ottawa: Information Canada, 1973.

Cook, John P.; McKennan, Robert A. "The Athapaskan Tradition: A View from Healy Lake in the Yukon-Tanana Upland." Paper read by Robert A. MacKenna at the 10th annual meeting of the Northeastern Anthropological Association, Ottawa, May 7-9, 1970.

Dawson, George Mercer. *Notes on the Indian tribes of the Yukon District and Adjacent Northern Portion of British Columbia*. Montreal: Reprint from: Annual report of the Geological Survey of Canada, 191B-213B, 1887.

Dawson, George Mercer. *Notes on the Shuswap People of British Columbia*. From Transactions of the Royal Society of Canada, section III, 1891. Original and microfiche (CIHM Microfiche series; no. 14874).

Dawson, George Mercer. *The Journals of George M. Dawson: British Columbia, 1875-1878*, edited by Douglas Cole and Bradley Lockner: 2 volumes. Vancouver: University of British Columbia Press, 1989.

Guy, Camil. *Le canot d'ecorce a Weymontaching*. Ottawa: National Museums of Canada, 1970. National Museum of Man. Anthropological Studies; no. 20

Heriot, George. *Travels Through the Canadas, containing a description of the picturesque scenery on some of the rivers and lakes: with an account of the productions, commerce, and inhabitants of those provinces. To which is subjoined a comparative view of the manners and customs of several of the Indian nations of North and South America. Illustrated with a map and numerous engravings, from drawings made at the several places by the author*. Edmonton: Hurtig, 1971. Reprint of the 1807 edition with a new introduction by James J. Talman.

Kidd, Kenneth E. *Blackfoot Ethnography*. Thesis (M.A.), University of Toronto: 1937.

Larmour, W. T. Canada, Department of Indian Affairs and Northern Development. *The Art of the Canadian Eskimo*. Ottawa: Queen's Printer, 1967.

MacMillan, Donald Baxter. *Eskimo Place Names and Aid to Conversation*. Washington: Hydrographic Office, U.S. Navy, 1943.

Memoir (Geological Survey of Canada). Ottawa: Government Printing Bureau, 1910-. Irregularly published. Some volumes also published in French under title: Mémoire - Commission géologique du Canada.

Neville, G. W. *Linguistic and Cultural Affiliations of Canadian Indian Bands.* Ottawa: Indian Affairs & Northern Development, 1970.

Rasmussen, Knud; Moltke, Harald Viggo; Herring, G. *The People of the Polar North: A Record by Knud Rasmussen, Compiled from the Danish Originals and Edited by G. Herring.* Illustrations by Count Harald Moltke. London: K. Paul, Trench, Trubner & Co., 1908.

Speck, Frank Goldsmith. *Double-curve Motive in Northeastern Algonkian Art.* Ottawa: Government Printing Office, 1914. GSC Memoir 42. NMC Bulletin, Anthropological Series; no. 1.

Speck, Frank Goldsmith. *Timiskaming Indians: Family Hunting Territories and Social Life of Various Algonkian Bands of the Ottawa Valley. Myths and Folk-lore of the Temiskaming Algonquin and Timagami Ojibwa.* Ottawa: Government Printing Bureau, 1915. GSC Memoir 70/71, NMC Bulletin, Anthropological series; no. 8.

Speck, Frank Goldsmith. *Decorative Art of Indian Tribes in Connecticut.* Ottawa: Geological Survey, 1915. GSC Memoir 75, NMC Bulletin, Anthropological Series; no. 10.

Stanley, John Mix. *Portraits of North American Indians with Sketches of Scenery, etc. Painted by J.M. Stanley, Deposited with the Smithsonian Institution.* Washington: Smithsonian Institution, 1852. Original and microfiche (CIHM Microfiches series; no. 41958).

Symposium on Circumpolar Problems, 1969, Berg, Gosta. *Circumpolar Problems: Habitat, Economy, and Social Relations in the Arctic: A Symposium for Anthropological Research in the North, September, 1969.* Edited by Gosta Berg. Oxford: Pergamon Press, 1973.

Tolmie, W. Fraser; Dawson, George Mercer. *Comparative Vocabularies of the Indian Tribes of British Columbia, With a Map Illustrating Distribution.* Montreal: Dawson Brothers,1884.

Archaeology

Auger, Reginald. *Labrador Inuit and Europeans in the Strait of Belle Isle: from the Written Sources to the Archaeological Evidence.* Quebec: Centre d'etudes nordiques, Universite Laval, 1991.

Bielawski, E; Kobelka, Carolyn; Janes, Robert R. *Thule Pioneers.* Yellowknife: Prince of Wales Northern Heritage Centre, 1986. Occasional paper; no.2.

Campbell, John Martin. *Archeological Studies Along the Proposed Trans-Alaska Oil Pipeline Route.* Washington: Arctic Institute of North America (Technical paper; no. 26), 1973.

Capes, Katherine H. *The W.B. Nickerson Survey and Excavations, 1912-15, of the Southern Manitoba Mounds Region.* Ottawa: National Museum of Canada, 1963. Anthropology Papers; no. 4.

Cinq-Mars, Jacques. *Preliminary Archaeological Study, Mackenzie Corridor.* Ottawa: Information Canada, 1973. Report (Task Force on Northern Oil Development, Canada, Environmental-Social Committee) no. 73-10.

Cinq-Mars, Jacques. *Preliminary Archaeological Study, Mackenzie Corridor (Second report).* Ottawa: Information Canada, 1974. Report (Task Force on Northern Oil Development, Canada, Environmental-Social Committee) no. 74-11.

Cinq-Mars, Jacques. *Preliminary Archaeological Study, Mackenzie Corridor (Final report).* Ottawa: Information Canada, 1976. Series: North of 60; Indian and Northern Affairs. Series: INA publication; no. QS8095-000-EE-A1. Series: ALUR (Arctic Land Use Research Program); 74-75-92.

Dewdney, Selwyn H. *Dating Rock Art in the Canadian Shield Region.* Toronto, Royal Ontario Museum, 1970. Art & Archaeology occasional paper; 24.

Drier, Roy Ward; Du Temple, Octave Joseph. *Prehistoric Copper Mining in the Lake Superior Region: a Collection of Reference Articles*. Calumet, Michigan: R.W. Drier, 1961.

Fitzhugh, William W. *Environmental Archeology and Cultural Systems in Hamilton Inlet, Labrador: A Survey of the Central Labrador Coast from 3000 B.C. to the Present*. Washington: Smithsonian, 1972.

Fladmark, Knut R. *A Paleoecological Model for Northwest Coast Prehistory*. Ottawa: National Museums of Canada, 1975. Paper - Archaeological Survey of Canada; no. 43.

Johnston, Richard B. *Archaeology of Rice Lake, Ontario*. Ottawa: National Museum of Canada, 1968. Anthropology papers; no. 19.

Lasca, Norman P.; Donahue, Jack. *Archaeological Geology of North America*. Boulder: Geological Society of America, 1990. Series; Decade of American Geology, Centennial special volume; 4.

Petitot, Emile; Fortune, Stanislas Joseph. *The Amerindians of the Canadian Northwest in the 19th Century, As Seen by Emile Petitot*. Edited by Donat Savoie. Ottawa: Northern Science Research Group, Indian Affairs and Northern Development, 1970. Mackenzie Delta Research Project. MRDP; 9-10.

Reeves, Brian O. K. *Crowsnest Pass Archeological Project*. Ottawa: National Museum of Man, 1974. Paper, Archeological Survey of Canada; no. 19, 24.

Schledermann, Peter; Jenness, Diamond. *Thule Eskimo Prehistory of Cumberland Sound, Baffin Island, Canada*. Ottawa: National Museums of Canada, 1975. Paper - Archaeological Survey of Canada; no. 38.

Solecki, Ralph S.; Jacobson, Jerome; Salwen, Bert. *Archaeological Reconnaissances North of the Brooks Range in Northeastern Alaska*. Calgary: University of Calgary Dept. of Archaeology, 1973. Occasional papers; no.1.

Webb, Clarence H. *The Poverty Point Culture*. Baton Rouge: Louisiana State University, School of Geoscience, 1982.

Workman, William B.; Jenness, Diamond. *Prehistory of the Aishnik-Kluane Area, Southwest Yukon Territory*. Ottawa: National Museums of Canada, 1978. paper, Archaelogical Survey of Canada; no. 74.

Wright, James Vallière. *The Prehistory of Lake Athabaska: An Initial Statement*. Ottawa: National Museums of Canada, 1975. paper, Archaeological Survey of Canada; no. 29.

History, Exploration and First Encounters

Canadian Arctic Expedition. *Report of the Canadian Arctic Expedition, 1913-18*. Ottawa:. Conference reports: v.12— The Copper Eskimos; v.13—Eskimo Folk-lore; v.14 Eskimo Songs; v.15—Eskimo Language and Technology; Eskimo Language; v.16 — Material Culture of the Copper Eskimo.

Farquar, Julia, Arctic Awareness Program. *Following His Father's Footsteps: Stuart Jenness Travels to Coppermine*. Ottawa: EMR, 1989.

Hall, Charles Francis. *Life With the Esquimaux: A Narrative of Arctic Experience in Search of Survivors of Sir John Franklin's Expedition*. Rutland: C.E. Tuttle Co., 1970. Reprint of the 1865 edition, with a new introduction by George Swinton.

Hall, Charles Francis. *Narrative of the Second Arctic Expedition Made by Charles F. Hall: his voyage to Repulse Bay, sledge journeys to the straits of Fury and Hecla and to King William's land and residence among the eskimos during the years 1864-69*. Edited by J.E. Nourse. Washington: Government Printing Office, 1879.

Hantzsch, Bernard Adolph; Neatby, Leslie H. *My life Among the Eskimos: Baffinland journeys in the Years 1909 to 1911*; translated from the German original and edited by Leslie H. Neatby. Saskatoon: University of Saskatchewan, 1977.

Hearne, Samuel. *A Journey from Prince of Wales' Fort in Hudson's Bay to the Northern Ocean, Undertaken by Order of the Hudson's Bay Company for the Discovery of Copper Mines, a North West Passage, &c., in the Years 1769, 1770, 1771, & 1772*. Edmonton: Hurtig, 1971. New edition.

Henry, Alexander. *Travels and Adventures in Canada and the Indian territories, Between the Years 1760 and 1776*. Edited with notes by James Bain. Rutland: C.E. Tuttle Co., 1969. First published in 1809.

Hind, Henry Yule. *Narrative of the Canadian Red River Exploring Expedition of 1857 and of the Assiniboine and Saskatchewan Exploring Expedition of 1858*. Winnipeg: Hurtig, 1971. Reprint of 1860 edition.

Hooper, William Hulme. *Ten Months Among the Tents of the Tuski: with incidents of an Arctic boat espedition in search of Sir John Franklin, as far as the Mackenzie River and Cape Bathurst*. London: John Murray, 1853.

Klutschak, Heinrich. *Overland to Starvation Cove, With the Inuit in Search of Franklin, 1878-1880*. Translated and edited by William Barr. Toronto: University of Toronto Press, 1987.

Low, A. P. *Report on the Dominion Government Expedition to Hudson Bay and the Arctic Isalnds On Board the D.G.S. Neptune, 1903-1904*. Ottawa: Government Printing Bureau, 1906.

MacDonald, Robert. *The Uncharted Nations: A Reference History of the Canadian Tribes*. Calgary: Ballantrae Foundation, 1978. Series - The Romance of Canadian History; 3.

Mackenzie, Alexander. *Voyages from Montreal on the River St. Laurence Through the Continent of North America to the Frozen and Pacific oceans in the Years 1789 and 1793: with an account of the rise, progress and present state of the fur trade of that country*. Edmonton: Hurtig, 1971. Also New York: New Amsterdam Book Company, 1902. Also London: T. Cadell and W. Davies, 1801.

Mair, Charles; MacFarlane, Roderick. *Through the Mackenzie Basin: A Narrative of the Athabaska and Peace River Treaty Expedition of 1899; also notes on the mammals and birds of northern Canada*. London: Simpkin, Marshall, Hamilton, Kent, 1908.

McCutcheon, Sean. *Electric Rivers: The Story of the James Bay Project*. Montreal: Black Rose, 1991.

Northern Co-ordination and Research Centre. NCRC Series. Ottawa: Northern Affairs and National Resources, 1957 -. Holdings: 57-1 -61-4, 61-6 -63-5, 63-1 -67-2.

Parker, Samuel. *Journal of an exploring tour beyond the Rocky Mountains, under the direction of the A.B.C.F.M. in the years 1835, '36, and '37 containing a description of the geography, geology, climate, productions of the country, and the numbers, manners, and customs of the natives, with a map of Oregon Territory*. Ithaca: Mack, Andrus & Woodruff, 1842. 3rd edition, original and microfiche. (CIHM Microfiche series; no. 41949).

Parry, Sir William Edward. *Journal of a second voyage for the discovery of a north-west passage from the Atlantic to the Pacific; performed in the years 1821-22-23, in his majesty's ships Fury and Hecla, under the Orders of Captain William Edward Parry, R.N., F.R.N., and Commander of the expedition/ published by authority of the Lords Commissioners of the Admiralty/ accompanied by: Appendix to Captain Parry's journal of the second voyage for the discovery of a north-west passage from the Atlantic to the Pacific...* London: John Murray, 1824 (Appendix: 1825).

Peary, Robert. *Northward Over the Great Ice: a narrative of life and work along the shores and upon the interior ice-cap of Northern Greenland in the years 1886 and 1891-1897, with a description of the little tribe of Smith Sound Eskimos, the most northerly human beings in the world, and an account of the discovery and bringing home of the Saviksue or great Cape York meteorites.* London: Methuen, 1898.

Price, Ray. *The Howling Arctic: The Remarkable People Who Made Canada Sovereign in the Farthest North.* Toronto: P. Martin, 1970.

Rasmussen, Knud. *Across Arctic America: Narrative of the Fifth Thule Expedition.* New York: G.P. Putnam's Sons, 1969. Translation of *Fra Gronland til Stillehavet.*

Steffansson, Vilhjalmur. *The Friendly Arctic: The Story of Five Years in Polar Regions.* New York: Greenwood Press, 1943. New edition with new material.

Sutton, George Miksch. *Eskimo Year: A Naturalist's Adventures in the Far North; illustrated with drawings and photographs by the author and photographs by several men of the north country.* New York: The Macmillan Co, 1934.

Tweedsmuir, John Norman Stuart Buchan. *Hudson's Bay Trader.* New York: Norton, c1951. 1st American edition.

Tyrrell, James Williams. *Across the Sub-arctics of Canada: A Journey of 3,200 miles by Canoe and Snow-shoe Through the Barren Lands.* Toronto: Coles Publishing Co., 1973 (Coles Canadiana Collection). Also: London: T. Fisher Unwin, 1897. Also: Toronto: William Briggs, 1897.

Wentzl, Jan; Valenta, Edvard; Golombek, Bedrich. *Thirty Years in the Golden North;* translated by Paul Selver. New York: Macmillan, 1932.

Maps

Allen, R.S; Maguire, R. *Canada, Indian Treaties.* Energy Mines & Resources Canada. National Atlas of Canada 5th ed.; MCR 4162.

British Columbia Treaty Commission. *Traditional Territories of British Columbia First Nations.* G.M. Johnson and Associates Ltd.: British Columbia Treaty Commission, 1994.

Heidenreich, Conrad E. *Canada, Native Peoples 1630.* Ottawa: Energy Mines & Resources Canada, 1988. National Atlas of Canada 5th ed.; MCR 4054.

Heidenreich, Conrad E. *Canada, Native Peoples 1740.* Ottawa: Energy Mines & Resources Canada, 1988. National Atlas of Canada 5th ed.; MCR 4094.

Heidenreich, Conrad E. *Canada, Native Peoples 1823.* Ottawa: Energy Mines & Resources Canada, 1988. National Atlas of Canada 5th ed.; MCR 4139.

Jost, I. *Canada, Indian and Inuit communities and Languages.* Ottawa: Energy Mines & Resources Canada, 1980. National Atlas of Canada 5th ed.; MCR 4001. Includes ancillary maps, graphs and list of bibliographic sources.

Jost, I. *Canada, Indian and Inuit Population Distribution.* Ottawa: Energy Mines & Resources Canada. National Atlas of Canada 5th ed.; MCR 4031.

National Geographic Society. *Native American Heritage: A Visitors Guide.* Washington: National Geographic Society, 1991. Includes ancillary maps, notes and illustrations.

Wentzel, Willard Ferdinand. *Mackenzie River With a Map.* In manuscript, signed; W.F. Wentzel, Expedition House, named Fort Enterprise on Winter Lake, Febr. 20th, 1821. Original and microfiche (CIHM Microfoche series; no. 41960).

Policy and Politics

Bone, Robert M. *The Geography of the Canadian North: Issues and Challenges.* Toronto: Oxford University Press, 1992.

Committee for Original Peoples' Entitlement. *The Western Arctic Claim: The Inuvialuit Final Agreement.* Ottawa: Indian and Northern Affairs Canada, 1984.

Dacks, Gurston. *A Choice of Futures: Politics in the Canadian North.* Toronto: Methuen, 1981.

Ferguson, J.D. *The Human Ecology and Social and Economic Change in the Community of Tuktoyaktuk, N.W.T.* Ottawa: Northern Co-ordination and Research Centre, Northern Affairs and National Resources, 1961.

Inuit Circumpolar Conference. *Principles and Elements for a Comprehensive Arctic Policy.* Montreal: Centre for Northern Studies and Research, McGill University, 1992. Compilation of all the principles approved at ICC General Assemblies and additional draft principles prepared to date.

Jenness, Diamond. *Eskimo Administration:* I. *Alaska* (Technical paper 10); II. *Canada* (Technical paper 14); III. *Labrador* (Technical paper 16); IV. *Greenland* (Technical paper 19). Montreal: Arctic Institute of North America, 1962.

Wojciechowski, Margot J.; Graham, Katherine A. *Sourcebook for Native Participation in Canadian Mineral Activities.* Kingston: Centre for Resource Studies, Queen's University, 1985. Technical Paper - Centre for Resource Studies; no. 5.

ACCESS

Photographs

Photo Library
Earth Sciences Information Centre
601 Booth Street
Ottawa, ON K1A 0E8
Tel: (613) 996-9369
Fax: (613) 954-1109
URL: http://www.nrcan.gc.ca/gsc/
e-mail: plibrary@gsc.nrcan.gc.ca
Telnet: 132.156.35.177

The images in the photo library are available for private, educational and commercial use. Prints or slides may be ordered by mail, telephone, fax or e-mail. There are charges for reproduction, search time over fifteen minutes, and shipping and handling. A current fee schedule is available on request.

Photographs are identified by their call numbers. The images of native subjects have all been catalogued in the library's computer database, which can be searched on site or by Telnet from a remote site at 132.156.35.177. The catalogue can also be searched by author and subject, so related images and documents can be traced.

A large number of the Survey's earliest photographs, including many of native subjects, have been transferred to the custody of the National Archives, the Canadian Museum of Civilization and the Canadian Museum of Nature. Arrangements may be made with those institutions to search, view and acquire images.

National Archives of Canada
Reference Services
Tel: (613) 996-7797
Fax: (613) 995-6274
URL: http://www.archives.ca

Records of GSC photographs in the National Archives will be found in Finding Aid 16.

Canadian Museum of Civilization Library
Tel: (819) 776-8177
Fax: (819) 776-8491
e-mail: louis.campeau@cmcc.muse.digital.ca
Reference requests must be made in writing, but may be submitted by fax.

Canadian Museum of Nature
Librairies and Archives
Tel: (613) 998-3924
Fax: (613) 998-1065
e-mail: mboudreau@mus-nature.ca

For publishing rights, contact:
Tel: (613) 990-6671
Fax: (613) 990-0318

Documents

Earth Sciences Information Centre
601 Booth Street
Ottawa, ON K1A 0E8
Tel: (613) 996-3919
Fax: (613) 954-1109
URL: http://www.nrcan.gc.ca/gsc/
e-mail: library@gsc.nrcan.gc.ca
Telnet: 132.156.35.177

The documents in the library are available for loan, and copies of selected portions may be purchased. As with the photo library, there are charges for reproduction, searches over fifteen minutes, and shipping and handling. A current fee schedule is available from the library.

Most of the document collection is catalogued in a computer database, and can be accessed on-site or by Telnet from a remote site at 132.156.35.177. The catalogue can be searched by author, title, call number, document type and subject.

The Geological Survey has a Web site, http://www.nrcan.gc.ca/gsc/esic/esic_e.html (English) or http://www.nrcan.gc.ca/gsc/esic/esic_f.html (French), which provides up-to-date information on earth science subjects and events, and access to the electronic library catalogues.

Index of Photographs